Footprints in the Sand

A collection of poetry

Yameen Subhan Rahman

ISBN: 978-1721212620

© Yameen Subhan Rahman 2018

All rights reserved. No part of this publication may be reproduced,
distributed, or transmitted in any form or by any means,
including photocopying, recording, or other electronic or mechanical methods,
without the prior written permission of the publisher,
except in the case of brief quotations embodied in critical reviews and
certain other non-commercial uses permitted by copyright law.
For permission requests, email the publisher at the address below.

E: yameen2004@gmail.com
E: jrahman2@hotmail.co.uk

Dedicated to my beloved grandparents.

Missing you always.

Praise for Yameen...

"...Yameen Rahman displays a remarkable maturity in his poems. His use of language and his perceptions are impressive in one so young and he both writes and speaks with a confidence and intelligence not often found in his peers. Well done, Yameen!" **Dr. Martin Parker**, Associate Professor, University of Bahrain.

"Yameen is a young poet with the heart and mind of a mature adult. He has a natural sense of rhythm and imagery and a delightful ability at personification. He has a low-key personality and when he joined the Bahrain Writers' Circle in 2016, he surprised us older poets with the strength of his quiet delivery. Over the past two years as a BWC member and participant in the group's annual Colours of Life poetry festival (2016 & 2017) the quality of his poems has improved and his insight sharpened. I look forward to watching Yameen hone his craft, he has tremendous potential and someday I hope to see his name in lights." **Rohini Sunderam**, author, writer, poet, President of The Bahrain Writers' Circle.

"Yameen Rahman's quiet style is reflected in his descriptive poetry. It is delightful to read the rhythm in his candid poems and dwell on how this talented young poet perceives the world around him. The youngest member of the Bahrain Writers' Circle, Yameen gives us hope that the 'word' is still alive in the younger generation" **Mobeena Inam**, writer and poet.

"I first met Yameen Rahman when he was a young 11 year old, during one of the poetry evenings of the Bahrain Writers Circle in Manama, in early 2016. We were preparing for the 2016 Colours of Life festival, where individual poets of various nationalities, ages and skill set levels, present one or more of their original poems to a small audience. I remember being struck by this young man's skill and confidence even then, at that tender age. I was delighted to hear Yameen confidently present two more of his poems a year later, in the 2017 edition of Colours of Life in Manama. I wish him continued success with his creative writing." **Cyrus Dali Vesuvala**, singer, songwriter and poet.

"Yameen is a young poetic prodigy whose passion for story-telling is matched by the courage to perform shoulder to shoulder with his adult peers. Proving that even a little man has something to say about a world riddled with adults." **Omar Ahmed Khulaqi**, poet.

"Yameen is an excellent poet, and his poems demonstrate a high level of sophistication and his love of writing." **Mr. Scissions,** Yameen's former teacher at the St. Christopher's School, Bahrain.

"Yameen Rahman has been with Drama Scene since 2016 (Ductac Mall of Emirates) As a young boy growing up in Saudi Arabia, Bahrain and currently in Dubai, as well as a frequent traveller, Yameen's poetry vastly reflects his experiences. Yameen began training under the LAMDA syllabus in Bahrain where he has continued through his grades, currently working towards his Solo Acting Grade 3 examination in Dubai. Yameen writes with depth; with emotion and passion. It is evident that his experience on stage is a huge asset in his writing and wonderful to see how much they work hand in hand together. A young man with a bright future ahead of him!" **Emma Quintin** - Head Teacher of LAMDA (London Academy of Music & Dramatic Art).

"I have been acquainted with Yameen's poetry for a couple of years now - he has a unique sensitivity for someone so young, an impressive poetic voice. I particularly liked his performances at the Colours of life Poetry Festival in Bahrain, and that he flew in from UAE to present his poetry speaks volumes about his passion for his art. I wish him all the best for his journey ahead, it will be interesting to watch his pen mature and I am sure he will give much pleasure to his readers/audience in coming years." **Nilanjana Bose**, writer, poet, blogger.

"When I met Yameen the first time, it gave me such a joy to look at a young dashing boy's intention to join a Writers Circle. He was only 11 year old at that time. Then, when he presented his poems, I knew I was witnessing a future poet. It has been a pleasure to share the joy of poetry and the excitement of on stage poetry narration with Yameen, and wish him a bright future on writing and especially in poetry." **Lonita Nugrahaya**, poet.

"For someone so young, Yameen has a rare and extraordinary way with words. He displays a unique eloquence in his construction and composition of poetry and his ability in putting his thoughts and feelings onto paper in a fluid, structured and meaningful way. A poet laureate in the making!" **Robin Barratt**, author, writer & publisher, and founder of the Bahrain Writers' Circle.

About Yameen...

"One of the first poetry books I ever read was *A Year Full of Poems* by Michael Harrison and Christopher Stuart-Clark. I enjoyed the compilation of poems which explore diverse subjects that evoke deep emotions and a timeless reflection within the reader. Since then, I began to write and read poetry more often, as I enjoyed expressing my thoughts and imagination.

Poetry has enabled me to describe aspects both literally and metaphorically through being inspired by life experiences, literature and everyday language. I enjoy writing poetry because it warrants a sense of directness, creativity and accessibility whereby a carefully crafted poem of selected words and verses has the ability to explore a real depth of emotion and imagination within the reader so much more than writing prose. I feel a sense of satisfaction in being compelled to work with a minimalism of words whist trying to unravel limitless affairs of the heart and mind on paper.

On reflection, I tend to think creatively and wonder with imagination when I'm alone in a place devoid of distraction when an idea hits me! I believe it's John Keates who had said *'Poetry is like a leaf in the wind. If it does not come naturally, it should not come at all'*. I tend to write typically within my home, albeit of recent I have ventured into the outdoors, library and garden for inspiration.

As an aspiring writer, I hope to emulate my idols and compose poetry centred on contemporary themes, emotive ideas and historical events. I wish to discern a perspective within my poetry that reflect emancipation, hope and compassion once you've read the entire piece. I would also wish for my poems to relate to the reader on a more intellectual and purposeful level, rather than exhibiting pure imagination.

I have been an avid reader ever since I was a young age, and still am today! I started to read at age five, and went on to read books such as *Classic Starts* (a series of classic literature for children), *Goosebumps,* and widely known authors such as Roald Dahl and Charles Dickens. I have read of recent novels such as *Great Expectations, 20,000 Leagues under the Sea* and *Frankenstein*, which were a pleasure to read as I appreciated the depth of character profiling and breadth of genre which I try to represent and instil in my writing today. Currently, I have almost concluded reading the full *Harry Potter 7 book series, and am enjoying the Goblet of Fire in particular*. I enjoy reading the J.K Rowling's series as it concocts a range of interesting and compelling characters within the storyline, and one is enticed to turn the page until finished. After I complete reading *Goblet of Fire,* I would like to perhaps read Stephen King's *Cujo* or *Pet Cemetery*.

At present, I have embarked on writing on a short science-fiction / fantasy novel that will appeal to ages 11- 17. I've finished a few drafts of the first chapter and am working to formalise the plot and outline. I hope to complete the novel as a hobby, while maintaining my focus on my academic studies. I wish to eventually study either biomedical engineering, neurology, history or another science-based field at degree level. These choices are of course prone to change as I am still young. After my university studies, I hope to embrace a respectable profession and ensure I prosper from there.

Finally, I sincerely thank and appreciate my readers and family for all their good will, encouragement and sentiment shown over the years."

Yameen Subhan Rahman
February, 2018

CONTENTS

	PAGE
Foreword by David Hollywood.	10
A Poem.	12
The Blind Men.	13
The Camel.	14
The River of Tajpur.	15
The Lantern.	16
The Moon.	17
Gollum.	18
The Mountain Climber.	19
The Owl.	20
The Rice Woman.	21
The Wise Man's Nonsense.	22
I am the King.	23
'3'	24
Ents.	25
Entertain Me.	26
Dubai.	27
21/11/71.	28
Richard I: 'The Lion Heart.	29
The Cheeky Old Cat.	30
Walking On The Moon.	31
My Grandma's Garden.	32
An Expat Life.	33
The Bull.	34
The Living Room.	35
The Monster of Skimwick.	36
The Black Death.	37
A Rather Amusing Monkey.	38
To Live a Life.	39
Love.	40
Missing You.	41
Summer Winds.	42
The Other Side.	43
Breakfast.	44
Gandalf.	45
Throughout the Hot Astir and to the Silent Night.	46
Thinking.	47
Footprints.	48

Ghosts of the Past.	49
Happiness.	50
Lies.	51
Hey Sister!	52
My lovely Dada Bhai.	53
The Great Tale of Greeteus – *a short tale.*	55

Foreword by David Hollywood

"I met Yameen when he attended a number of poetry workshops being sponsored by his school in Bahrain, and quickly came to realise his talent for the written word was of a standard beyond his years.

In addition to demonstrating a great commitment to poetry, he engaged wonderfully with the rest of his peers, plus myself, in being able to present to us all the benefits of delivering a poem according to its sentiments and intention. After a short time being instructed and guided in how to best use tone, inflection and voice projection Yameen was able to convert and lift his words from the page and into the ears and minds of the audience, so that once received, the meaning and sense of feeling emanating from his script became something to be felt and understood.

This is a difficult accomplishment for a person so young, but Yameen was an attentive and conscientious learner.

However, none of this would have meant much beyond performance if it were not for the sense of description contained within Yameen's poetry writings. I was surprised and very impressed to read such mature descriptions of the world around us through his observations of the human condition and circumstances in which we work and play, and to then have this complimented by wonderfully sensitive appreciations of the animal kingdom and environment, proved to us all that what is within Yameen is a terrifically natural gift and talent to place together harmonies which touch our esoteric sense of enjoyment and understanding.

Yameen is an unassuming young poet who says little about his efforts but overflows with his written descriptive powers, and consequently I believe he shall enjoy great admiration from his readers. He can look forward to impressive prospects with his writings, and it shall be wonderful to watch his progression and read his undiscovered works of the future. I wish him every success with his skills and hope whoever sees his works enjoys them as much as I have." **David Hollywood -** *Founding member of The Bahrain Writers' Circle, Chairman of The Second Circle poetry group, and director of The Colours of Life poetry festival.*

Footprints in the Sand

A Poem

A poem is one that evokes emotion and thought,
Steeped in a discovery of many shapes and faces,
A measure of wonder, abstract and valour.

A poem is one that forges ideas and views,
A sonnet, rhyme, riddle or ode that brings new meaning,
And illuminates the essence of life and reason.

A poem is one that brings life to a distant shore,
Imparting truth of a world rich in shade and colour,
A testament to man's spirit to forever endure.

The Blind Men
Dedicated to the lost souls of WW1

Our legs trembling,
Our feet burning,
As our backs ache with sweat.
Our eyes blackened,
Our ears thickened,
As our rifles were soon to be set.
Our heads laced with fever,
Our hearts entrenched with fear,
As our tears run dry once wet.
Our fingers slender,
Our mouths tender,
As our demise was soon to be met.

The Camel

There amongst the sand dunes of gold,
Where the deepest of footprints seem to move over time,
A boiling-hot sun that smiles upon earth with no worry at all,
In the excruciating sunlight, a camel standing tall.

"Farewell," the camel said, *"it is time to leave the desert,*
Goodbye my sun that gave me sweat,
And sandstorms that paint the landscape within my very eyes.
However my friends, Khan the Great, I hear his cries"

There amongst the green of forests,
Where the fragrance of animals disseminate in quick,
And the wise camel continues his journey, but for the pain and crick,
His feet eventually grew tired with the sharp twigs and sticks.

"Farewell," the camel said, *"it is time to leave the forest,*
Goodbye my fellow trees that gave me shelter,
And the flies that lived upon my very eyes,
However my friends, Khan the Great, I hear his cries."

There amongst the black of mountains,
Fear and trepidation heighten my doubts,
As the scary wolves howl and shout,
The wise camel journeying through Bahrain,
Passing tempests of wind, and the gibes of rain.

"Farewell," the camel said, *"it is time to leave the mountains,*
Goodbye my stone that let me walk
And the dust that concealed my very eyes,
However my friends, Khan the Great, I hear his cries."

The River of Tajpur

The fisherman lives an honest life, worthy of God's command,
An unyielding stream of harmony that separates both lands.
Deep beneath the river, lies soil enriched with history,
Ancestors of our fathers, there lives a forgotten mystery.

Talapiya run wild and free, embracing the imperious sun,
As night beckons and Azan escapes, waters run empty and numb.
And as rigid and timeless stones lie innocent and cold,
Larva of a mosquito begins to breed new life and gently unfold.

The Lantern

Red lighted lanterns, that assist us in the dark,
And the fire it emits, ignites an orange spark.
Those who are lost, take no concern,
As lanterns share light and shadows it burns.

Red lighted lanterns, that reveal spirits of light,
And the fire it emits, takes you beyond the night.
Those who are lost, take no concern,
As lanterns share light and shadows it burns.

The Moon

The Moon walks across a path of cloud and grey,
Each night she follows and protects me as I wonder and stray.
And as she gleams like a silver coin melting in the sun,
The moon is a ghostly galleon out on the run.

The moon smiles back at earth as the distant stars embrace,
Each night I stare at her craters assembled as an old weathered face.
The moon is a timeless guardian of wisdom and splendour,
Looking out over all of us, as gravity pulls us ever closer.

Gollum

For Sméagol, things were never the same,
A pale white being consumed by a ring that devoured the weak.
An extraordinary power that he could never control nor claim,
As he yearned for knowledge that the blind men seek.

For five hundred years, Gollum possessed the ring,
Sauron's magic spread like a prevailing sting,
All those years ago, when Sméagol choked his cousin to death,
His life turned into a sudden curse,
Now rotten fish on Gollum's sordid breath.

The Mountain Climber

An exhausted climber staggered,
Towards the summit through much fortitude,
With legs of agony and pain,
Snow drifted from the top, arriving towards him,
As an abundance of breeze rustled the leather he was wearing.

"Almost there," he shrieked;
And with a tremendous push, the climber made it!
An eruption of joy had healed him.
After leaping with much contentment, landing on his two very feet, the climber avowed, *'I have done it.'*

The Owl

The chilling wind casts a haunting breeze,
As the barren land snuggles to avoid her freeze.
And there awaits, a patient and solemn owl,
With piercing eyes forever on the night prowl.

Insects and worms scurry the winter grass in fear,
As the owl locks onto its meal with precision and spear.
Peaceful and quiet the landscape though it seems,
Predators and wolves scavenge in teams.

Jackdaw, cockerels and hedgehogs welcome the crimson sun,
In the dusk of the valley, as the owl's work is now done.
The night watchman retreats as she's no longer needed for now,
Until such time when darkness falls and sun takes a bow.

The Rice Woman

By the river bank, by the farm,
The rice woman passes like a spark of glistening charm,
As she glances back, brown hazelnut eyes of twinkle and wonder.
By the lake, by the harvest,
Rice for her starving children, acts of pure kindness.

And now the destitute stranger, a concealed enigma,
Still walks by me in the skies above,
The rice she carried, harvested out of tender and love.
By the village, by the sea,
I remember her as she would remember me.

The Wise Man's Nonsense

The wise old man spoke of nothing but absolute nonsense. With grey streaks of hair and wrinkles entrenched within his insipid face, the wise old man shared his words of absolute nonsense:

"Wouldn't it be terrific if you could leap from mountain to mountain and follow a rainbow, as winged purple hippos follow you home? Imagine if the slightest touch of light immersed you in wonder and beauty where ducklings sing songs and courgettes gigged with hedgehogs? Imagine if you could hold onto your most endearing memories, thoughts and emotions within a pile of goodness, to be transported away and called upon through the chambers of your brain! God that's heavenly!"

And that was the day, the day of the wise man's absolute nonsense.

I am the King

Indignation of Charles I towards Parliament on his beheading in 1649.

I am the King and thou shall kneel before me,
Like thy fathers did to predecessors of mine,
You cannot kill what you cannot see,
I am the King that binds man and time.

Twas I who was destined to rule over this great land,
And while I am adorned in gold and bless,
Know that with my demise you end the life you live today,
With a changing landscape devoid of order and conquest.

This hatred, resentment and animosity,
Shall bring nothing of prosperity or equality,
For no man but I can govern these lands,
As you shall now bear witness to blood and anarchy.

'3'
Inspired by Eleanor Rigby, Beatles, 1966

A youthful woman, in her filthy attire, picked up some rice where a wedding had been - her days encapsulated in others.
No one would talk to her.

Eleanor wondered through a long stretch until her satin cheeks rested against the window, wearing away a face mould, which deceived many fellows in her time.

A shallow time...

She squinted through the panes of her household, past the green hillocks and into some church grounds.

There.

"Look at him working."

Father McKenzie was sat by a tomb, darning his socks under a cornflower evening haze; he was only ever watched by two beings, one flesh - one supernatural...

Eleanor slept that night with her face mould in a jar, dreaming about a divine acquaintance of whom would take her about.
Her happiness buried in soils of tears.

To the other side of her bed, were sermons Father Mckenzie had written that no one would dare hear.

Lonesome.

2 weeks passed and Eleanor Rigby had silently unsealed her gift of agony. She cruised with one prayer as Father Mckenzie wiped dirt off his hands, sauntering from the new grave.

Silently.

Ents

Towering giants stand tall in peace,
They are neither monster nor enemy, but talking trees,
Standing tall are the guardians of the Fangorn forest,
Standing tall are the mighty Ents.

Slow but wise, creatures of knowledge they seem,
They are like the friends that guide your inner dreams,
Protectors of distant lands, they are the Ents.
Towering giants stand tall unto the weeds.

They bare no threat, harm or kill these talking trees,
Voices that relax, sooth and calm,
Love and time remain within their palm,
They are my friends, the Ents of wooded charm.

Entertain Me

Play the grandest, finest flute, and whistle away
Until my conscience escapes me.
Mesmerise me with the most vibrant and colourful of dances
As all my inhibitions leave me.
Perform the most revolutionary and enthralling drama
Which lifts me up and beckons me.
Sing the most melodic, harmonic of songs
That mystifies and immerses me.
Jump from the hardened cliffs of the past,
Into a sea of dreams that inspire me.
Entertain me so as within a moment of time,
I can finally breathe and feel alive.

Dubai

Busy, hectic, vast and loud,
Commercial, rich and colossal crowds,
Tradition lost and labour frowned,
Sky Scrapers high-to astound.

Luxury, sports cars, wealth at its peak,
Desserts, dunes, sands at our feet,
Arabic foods and sizzling meats,
Foreigners adore the country they seek.

Malls, resorts and water parks,
Traffic ahead, but fun at dark,
Construction close and buildings sparks,
Success they have but faith at heart.

21/11/71

Inspired by the Mitro Bahini struggle during Bangladesh independence, 21 November 1971.

Christened within a soulless bunker of earth, soon to be his grave.
Hands held tightly to a recoilless rifle,
As an Indian war cry echoes and fades across the bloody landscape.
Eyes piercing in-between PT-76 tanks,
Violent elephants spray drops of justice through decimating trunks.
The retreat of two rivals, he shall not shoot,
For he is stunned. Mitro Bahini have won!

Richard I: 'The Lion Heart'

Two leaders, one King and one Sultan,
Both offer no concession for their Holy land,
A duty to absolve their many sins.
Both lands share a settlement in rocky sands,
An Arab kingdom in each other's vision.

Saladin, a leader too strong as he withstands
The insurgence of Richard, a king of distant lands
Who eventually suffers heavy losses to his horses and men,
And finally succumbs to a retreat with winds not in his ken,

Two leaders, one crusade and one conqueror;
A battle begins, both knowing the perils of failure.
Richard, both ridiculed and admired, makes way to Europe.
Where out of pain and misery, finally imprisoned and full of fear,
As ransom is demanded by a duke of Austria.

One Leader, much silver,
Out of force and wealth,
Richard is released to live.
The Lionheart, crowned a second time,
Returns to Normandy,
Never to return.

The Cheeky Old Cat

Well first of all, the cheeky old cat claimed he devoured on a rat,
However, to be precise, he was only dreaming that.

Then secondly, the cheeky old cat thought he was rather fat,
However, to be precise, he was only a slither of a cat.

And thirdly, the cheeky old cat assumed he talked to a ghost,
However, to be precise, it was only the morning post,

Lastly, the cheeky old cat shouted;
"Help! A monster is upon me, I am quite certain of that."
However to be precise, his furry tail had suddenly just snapped.

Walking On the Moon
Inspired by the band, Police.

I never thought space exploration,
Would be an occasion,
For public elation,
But now I'm living the dream in my own accommodation.

Released from reality station,
Give your heart and soul to the dark emancipation,
Zero gravity, skipping in admiration,
Staring into the stars, forget your worries or trepidations.

Feet don't hardly touch the ground - levitation,
Walking back from your house, sipping on relaxation,
Exhaling fumes of pink solitude and supplication,
Be careful not to float away, an alien awaits the occasion.

My Grandma's Garden

My Grandma's Garden means so much to me,
Celebrated my first birthday in wonder for all to see.

My Grandma's Garden full of trees and streams,
Feed my thoughts of pure and wonderful things.

Shiny coco bells, daffodils and daisies,
Blue satin sachets tied onto roses.

Whispering prayers to Grandma now passed on,
To keep this garden alive, and hear a bird's heavenly song.

An Expat Life

Goodbye Saudi,
Hello Bahrain,
The elation that unravels me,
As I meet new faces and tell them my name.

A fresh new start awaits me,
Among horses, stables and fuss,
And the welcoming from merchants,
Fine people to trust.

The Land of the Dilmun,
I wander what lies ahead,
New school, new friends and blistering sun,
Fine Arab food, attire and thin flat bread.

Goodbye Saudi,
Hello Bahrain,
Time to ride ancient dhows,
Through open blue seas we venture now.

The Bull

A Spanish bull unyielding by choice,
Majestic and perfect, she's nobody's fool,
Commanding a respect, grace and poise,
She struts the streets as some start to jeer and pull.

Horns locked in, the bull's ready to pounce,
Taking on the matador as he stands so proud,
The bull lets rip as he moves in for his prey,
A deep wounded gash, he will live another day.

The Living Room

The boredom of couches, bruised by seating of egotistic masters,
Books and books opened over a thousand times,
Iranian assembled carpets accustomed to its 'flat, casual life,'
Multi-coloured cushions scattered by the energetic child,
A chessboard lies still as a cougar spotted by a youthful boy,
Pictures and paintings reflecting memories of time passed by,
The luminous plasma swallowing attention of its relatives and family,
An elderly clock smiling at the corner as she tick-tocks continuously,
The collections of CDs so complex in variety,
Vibrant paintings crafted by an absence of artists,
A shoe stand, like a skyscraper, infatuated with shoes;
The glamour of PS3 controls, waiting to be played,
Windows conveying the same light it has ever since its construction,
Curtains, long and guarding the house from the prying universe,
The Living Room.

The Monster of Skimwick

Sloppy and crooked, like a starved and scrawny cat,
Its claws hooked with menacing eyes in this old shack,
Skimwick feared the old devil,
The devil whom knows only terror,
Terror that redefines a new evil.

Tragic and ominous like an omen new born,
A face so wrinkly and ears withdrawn,
Skimwick fears the old devil,
The devil which had made a pact,
With hell and all that is evil.

Yet the closer one looked, like a never ending riddle,
It was no monster, but full of fear and weakness,
Alone in this world, yearning for wielders of the fiddle,
Skimwick has no fear of the devil,
As it looked so scared and misunderstood,
Oh, call the duke, for its body lay dead.

The Black Death

I am a hot rash that is the enemy within,
I am the acne of the face of a dystopian earth,
I prey on human decay, I am man's living sin,
As I am a placid liquid that feasts upon this bloody corpse.

My life is a game of hide and seek,
Seeking for flesh or coiled brain tissue,
To chew on meat or marrow vociferously,
Hiding from conscience and visibility.

Every day I roam the wastelands of a body undone,
Staggering like a tribal dancer,
Death will be my awakening, my one and last supper.
I cannot escape it, much work to be done.

Deep within the heart, under the layers of this soul,
Lies ones true self, yet to unfold,
However this time, isolated and afraid,
I shall devour all remains until stone cold.

A Rather Amusing Monkey

A rather amusing monkey,
Once sang through jungles of wood,
Emerges from the a lonely tree,
And waits by farmers gates in search of food.
Once in abundance, but now obscured,
By man and the logging of days gone by,
He now needs wit and deception to survive,
As his fall from grace tells a thousand cries.
Yet as he winks at me with his cute, concerning eyes,
This witty old monkey would neither wilt nor bend,
As tears descend across his weathered face,
This amusing monkey, my beautiful friend.

To Live a Life

How can you fly but not to the sky?
How can you live when you will not love?
How can you die if you have not lived?

For we shall dare to dream and touch the sky,
To have lived a life where love takes flight,
Full of passion and purpose as I kiss you goodbye.

Love

Love is the pink flame that blazes at the centre of your heart,
Love is an indelible fabric, that refuses to be pulled apart,
From the dawn of man that lasts beyond our days,
Love lives forever and gives shelter to the rain.

Miss You

Day after day, I yearn to see you,
Time stood still at our last rendezvous,
Day after day, melancholy plays a part,
Pulls me down to the depths of an aching heart.

Day after day, I start to cry,
Yearning for each photo to come alive,
Day after day, I don't know where you are,
Somewhere out there, so very far.

Summer Winds

A summer sun casts a gentle haze,
As the young come alive and animals graze,
A time for summer winds to reappear,
In which the passing of winter vanquish any fear.

As a new age brings hope and dreams,
As waters bring life into rivers and streams,
A time for summer winds to bring fortune and feast,
A new page is turned with the gentlest of kiss.

The Other Side

I stroll through the garden where souls dine and meet,
Stories of the past in a time not seen,
Headstones are all that remain of lives beneath my feet,
Strangers for now until the day they will lay my wreath.

Breakfast

I stare at purity in a glass, all silk and white,
Baked to perfection, the smells entice and consume me,
Swanky pressed jam bring colour and glam,
As eggs of Eden bring balance to the day,
With an earthly coffee to stir dreams awake.

Gandalf

A shadow of a pointy hat,
Who slayed beasts and dragons,
Who learnt of wizardry and a magical force,
The white rider, the rider of the shadow fox horse.

The towering Gandalf,
Father of ages and wise trodden path,
Who shook the ground with his eternal staff,
Born to conquer and dispel evil's wrath.

Resurrected from the depths of time,
Who lead dwarfs and hobbits to light,
Who stood and watched every obscure night,
Standing mighty and tall, was Gandalf the white.

Throughout the Hot Astir and to the Silent Night

In all its cherishing light, and with angel's will,
As the butterflies flutter and time stands still,
O' Lord come to us and let us embrace your might,
As we dream of days of truth and hope,
Throughout the hot astir and to the silent night.

Thinking

I was thinking of happiness and time,
How man and worlds came from stars and space,
I was thinking what made the snow, clouds and rain,
And how it blew my mind, as I was part of the same.

I was thinking what drove the earth round the sun,
How the body works, how I move, walk and run.
And how love was planted within the gardens of my brain,
Yet man waged war though we were all the same.

Footprints

As the waves sharply cut through open sea,
Salt hits the rising orbit of the vivid air,
I struggle to climb up onto the distant shore,
As I follow the footprints of time and evolution,
My mind fills up with wonder and curiosity,
For I find dry land and man's endless ingenuity.

Ghosts of the Past

Ghosts of the past, a captive son,
Feed upon those held in treason,
Holding back future's voice of reason,
Never to break free of days gone past,
Yearn to be in the present, free in the moment.
To set a new course of tomorrow's tomorrow,
Never knowing the truth of a captive son,
Pressures of the past, a boy on the run.

Happiness

Anger is your own madness,
Laughter is forever joyous,
Contentment is the lasting smile of a young boy.
Learning is maturing and growing is becoming,
Happiness is to love and be loved.

Happiness is living the dream,
That everlasting glow on a mothers face,
Happiness is a bitter sweet taste.
To surrender is your only demise,
Happiness is in the trying for a new rise.

Lies

Where lies water an Arab would know,
Where lies dunes exposed to both mystic and sun,
Where lies ambition, built from man's dream and endeavour,
Where lies seas and the dhow in search of destiny,
Where lies pearls that feel like silk,
Where lies mosques, terminals of Islam,
Where lies enriched carpets assembled by women of colour,
Where lies the camel and the ever constant wind and sun,
Where lies remain forbidden, and where good is taught,
For the Arabian lands of truth shall always be sought.

Hey Sister!

I love you just like a precious rose!
So delicate, pure and innocent,
And then there's that button like nose.

You are a special friend and shining star,
My heart is with you wherever you are.
Safiya, you are the pride of this young boy,
Before you grow older, our childhood we must enjoy!

My Lovely Dada Bhai

I looked after my Dadabai, with tender love and care,
He was with me in my younger life, and wise words he would share.
Handsome, studious and affable, my Dadabai was to me,
As I cry standing next to his exceptional grave,
And say prayers of love for my granddad to be safe.
The obscure night brings a deep rooted melancholy,
But the only light I see is Dadabai standing next to me.

The Great Tale of Greeteus
A short tale

Greeteus and his brother, Amuleus, were waiting to be registered for the Coliseum Night of Gladiators. The two brothers were known for their mighty hearts and great kindness. As they walked up to the Ring Master, Greeteus requested his gladiator fight to commence.

"Is that your brother there? The schedule states that Amuleus should participate in the Coliseum first, and then you thereafter", the Ring Master replied. Greeteus then turned to Amuleus to exclaim "Okay! Amuleus are you ready for this fight; remember what Dad taught us!"

"Greeteus, give me luck brother!", Amuleus responded, as he entered the stage and inhaled.

Greeteus ran upstairs to the highest view to watch his older brother battle. He believed in his strong and valiant Amuleus. However, Greeteus soon realized the opponent was Domules, the most successful and callous gladiator of all time! Tears ran down his cheeks, as he knew that Amuleus may die. Domules had slayed their own beloved father, a Roman General, many moons ago. From that day on, Romans began to fear him as much as Jupiter, the Roman God of Lightning.

After a brutal and dramatic battle, Domules inflicted a fatal wound on Amuleus who eventually died. Greeteus cried with sadness that spread across his face. However, there was no time to cry and be miserable. His own gladiator fight was about to commence.

After an intense battle, Greeteus had won his event. Greeteus was the stronger and more skilful of the two brothers. Despite winning, he ran straight out of the Coliseum without his gold trophy, and sat in an abandoned corner. As he reflected on his childhood with Amuleus, a sad and tearful Greeteus began to fall asleep.

The next morning, Greeteus was awoken by the tempest streets. He then saw a large placard that read: 'Rametorium Arena - Challenges tonight with the great Domules'.

"I've got to attend this!" cried Greeteus.

The night came soon enough. "Ah, your name is Greetues; I had a fun time with your brother!", Domules exclaimed. "Yes, that is my name; now I will have a fun time with you!", Greetues replied.

Greeteus demonstrated perfect skills. As time went by, Greeteus was now voted to battle against Domules! Greeteus accepted this challenge.

The challenge was about to start. Now it was Greeteus's chance to exact revenge. Domules walked up to the arena with sharp frosty eyes that glared at Greeteus.

Greeteus striked Domules with an upper cut; Domules was wounded.

However, Greeteus then allowed Domules to rise up again which was an honest action. Greeteus was true and valiant to himself. However, in a split second, Domules ran like a raging bull with his spear whilst Greeteus's back was turned. This act was forbidden. Sadly, the brave and honourable Greeteus had fallen.

A year later, Greeteus and Amuleus were summoned by Jupiter in paradise. Jupiter proclaimed the two brothers to be Supreme Guardians of the Highest Heaven forever. The 'Guardians of Light' were forever grateful, and soon became famous legends within Roman Mythology forever more.

Printed in Great Britain
by Amazon